Early Lists

of

Frederick Countians

[Maryland]

1765-1775

F. Edward Wright

HERITAGE BOOKS
2019

HERITAGE BOOKS
AN IMPRINT OF HERITAGE BOOKS, INC.

Books, CDs, and more—Worldwide

For our listing of thousands of titles see our website
at
www.HeritageBooks.com

Published 2019 by
HERITAGE BOOKS, INC.
Publishing Division
5810 Ruatan Street
Berwyn Heights, Md. 20740

International Standard Book Number
Paperbound: 978-0-7884-4271-1

CONTENTS

INTRODUCTION

Persons were required to publish a description of cows, horses, or other livestock that strayed onto their property. In most instances the animals had distinguishable marks, such as notches in the ear, in the case of a cow or hog, and brands, in the case of a horse. Giving notice of these strays tended to remove any question of thievery on the part of the person now holding the animal. If the owner showed up to claim the animal he was expected to pay for its feed. The notices for Frederick County were recorded in a separate volume titled Estrays, and constitute a fairly large number of different citizens. The names of the persons "taking up" the stray (less the descriptions of the animals) are made available in this work in the interest of locating early settlers of the county.

The latter two lists in this work show names of persons for which rent was due. Many are non-residents, some who had moved away, died, or in some cases never lived in the county.

All of these lists have been rearranged alphabetically, with the exception of the petition on page 19.

The reader will find several books of interest in which early settlers are listed. Millard Milburn Rice recently compiled extracts from Judgement Records of the Frederick County Court for the period 1748-1765, titled This Was The Life (Genealogical Publishing Co., Inc., Baltimore 1984). Not included in his selections is the petition shown in this book on page 19 which was also taken from these Judgement Records.

For other lists of early settlers of Frederick County the reader is referred to the following: First Settlements of Germans in Maryland by Edward T. Schultz (1896, repr. 1976 by Ruth T. Gross, Miami, Fla.), The Pennsylvania-German in Maryland by Daniel Wunderlich Nead (publ. Lancaster, Pa, 1914, repr. Genealogical Publ. Co., Inc., Baltimore 1975, 1980), and J. Thomas Scharf's, History of Western Maryland (2 vols., repr. Genealogical Publ. Co. 1968). Other works of genealogical interest in Frederick County include the following: T.J.C. Williams' History of Frederick County (2 vols., 1910); Jacob Mehrling Holdcraft's Names in Stone: 75,000 Cemetery Inscriptions of Frederick County (Ann Arbor, Michigan, 1966, 2 vols.); Pastor Frederick Sheely Weiser's Records of Marriages and Burials in the Monocacy Church in Frederick County, Maryland, and in the Evangelical Lutheran Congregation in the City of Frederick, Maryland, 1743-1811 (Washington, D.C., 1972); Raymond B. Clark's, Frederick County, Maryland, Naturalizations, 1799-1850 (1974, St. Michaels, Md.); and F. Edward Wright's Western Maryland Newspaper Abstracts, vol. 1, 1786-1798 and vol. 2, 1799-1805 (Family Line Publications, Silver Spring, Md.).

Abbreviations use in this book include the following.

AA - Anne Arundel
addl - land in additional to that
 reported earlier
Balt - Baltimore

Chas - Charles
Pa - Pennsylvania
PG - Prince George's
Va - Virginia

F. Edward Wright
13405 Collingwood Terrace
Silver Spring, Maryland 20904

Thomas Affutt, near the Grate Fall on
  Pot'k. River Apr 25 74
Valentine Ailer, living near Joseph
  Woods Jr.'s Mill on Israels Creek
  Jun 13 74
Zackariah Allbaugh Jul 15 73
Elizabeth Allen Dec 8 72
Moses Allen Nov 8 74
John Allison Aug 14 69
Frederick Ambrose Apr 28 67;
  Aug 31 69
Elizabeth Anderson living about Perry
  Creek Hd May 5 74
Alexander Anderson, brought by his
  son William (father sick)
  May 23 66
Philip Angleburgher Jun 11 70
Dawalt Ankney Jan 15 73
John Ankrom (recorded his mark)
  Aug 6 65
Balser Arbough May 19 70
Daniel Arnolt May 3 74
Henry Ash Mar 17 72
Thomas Ash Sep 19 67
Charles Atkins Apr 20 68
Thomas Austin Sep 25 75
Benjamin Baggerly, living near Mr.
  Snowden's Manor Oct 31 68
Peter Bainbridge Mar 21 70
Peter Baker Oct 26 74; Nov 8 74
John Balinger Jan 26 75
Henry Baltzel May 5 73
John Barber Apr 2 74
John Barber, Junr Sep 8 68
John Barrick Aug 19 71
Peter Barrickman Jul 31 67
Walter Basil Oct 22 66
Samuel Bayard Jan 22 67
John Baylie Nov 16 68
William Baylie Sep 24 74
Edward Beading Nov 19 66
Basil Beall Sep 26 71; Dec 6 74
Brooke Beall May 11 75
Col. George Beall Jul 14 66
Elisha Beall May 28 67; Apr 2 74
George Beall Jun 16 67
John Beall Aug 15 74; Jun 25 66;
  Sep 24 70
Ninion Beall Jul 3 73
William Beall Nov 26 66; Jun 17 67
John Beall of Bennett's Creek
  Jun 4 72

Edward Beatton, lying in the upper
  end of the sugar land Jul 21 73
George Beckworth Jul 7 67
Peter Becraft Apr 29 73
George Becraft   Apr 27 75
George Becraft of Pipe Creek
  Jun 17 65
Thomas Beeding Aug 17 65
John Bellough Dec 20 71
Abraham Benjamin Aug 6 69
William Bentley May 12 72
John Blair Feb 29 68; Dec 18 71
George Bond May 7 65
Thomas Bonton, living in Frederick Co
  near John Branch Oct 6 70
Alexander Botler Jun 27 67
Thomas Bowles Jun 24 73
John Bowlon(?) son of Zech. May 27 72
Baltis Bowman Oct 18 73
Baltsor Bowman Jun 13 74
Henry Boydsell May 27 74
Hubortis Boys of Isreals Creek
  Jul 21 65
Jacob Brangle Nov 26 66
Robert Briscoe Apr 30 66
Richard Brooke Jun 14 73
William Brooks Dec 4 65
Antoney Brost Jul 18 67
Edward Brown Feb 26 68
Richard Brown Jun 18 66
William Buchanan Aug 15 69
Creek Budge Nov 25 73
Thomas Burgee Jun 20 75
Peter Burghart Feb 11 75
William Burton Jan 20 68
Elixander Butler Jun 26 69
Samuel Butt Oct 25 68
John Buxton Sep 13 74
Byall Jun 12 69
Anne Callorigs(?), living near Ogles
  on Owens Creek Sep 27 70
Leanard Cammel Aug 10 65
Capt. Eanos Campbell Jun 7 68
Kneas Campbell Nov 21 71
John Campbell of Lenganore Dec 21 65
Kneas Campbell, living at upper end
  of the Sugar Lands Jun 19 71
David Canden Sep 5 69
Evin Carmack, living near Little Pipe
  Creek Jun 15 68
Capt. Samuel Carrick May 25 65
James Carsey Jul 2 65

Shadrach Case Mar 24 75; Aug 29 71
John Casel Jan 13 75
John Cellars Jr. Mar 15 73
Ninean Chamberlain Dec 16 66
Nathen Chaney Jun 24 66
Samuel Chen Mar 20 66
William Chilton Nov 3 66
John Chisolm, and overseer, Joseph
     Jean Jan 6 66
Benjamin Chittey Nov 26 68
George Church Jul 25 66
Thomas Clagett Jun 15 65
Henry Clark May 26 69
Neal(e) Clark Jul 18 68; Jun 19 69
William Clark Dec 10 67
Oswald Clements Dec 18 71
Michael Cober (Coler?) Feb 4 66
James Coffy Jul 15 67
James Cole Apr 20 73
Richard Collins Nov 15 73
William Condon Dec 9 72
James Conn, son of Hugh Conn
     Jun 18 66
Stephen Constable Jan 1 72
Ambrose Cook Jul 1 69
Martin Coonce Apr 19 75
Mary Ann Cooper Jun 17 65
Henry Cork Feb 17 74
Robert Corsleble Oct 14 68
John Cottrel Mar 31 66
Jeremiah Covel Nov 29 68
Nehemiah Covell Jul 1 75
Christian Cox Jun 10 74
Ezekle Cox Dec 19 74
John Cox, living on Friends Creek in
     the South Mountain nr Province
     Line Jul 4
Richard Crabb Jan 23 75; Sep 4 86
Joseph Craycraft Nov 19 66
Christian Creegar of Manocacy Manor,
     recorded by his wife Mary Aug 10
Christian Creeger Jul 11 68
Peter Creger Feb 20 68
Peter Crider Jun 2 73
Jacob Crook Jan 29 70
Charles Crouch Jun 12 72
Michael Crouse, living on Monocacy
     Manor Jul 29 69
Devault Crowley May 19 74
William Crum Sep 13 70
William Cumming Jun 2 67
George Curch (Carch?) Jul 25 68

Jacob Darner Aug 19 71
Abraham Davenport Nov 3 74
Charles Davis Jul 4 66
Gerrard Davis Oct 14 67; n.d.
Leonard Davis Oct 6 69; Jun 4 71
Richard Davis Aug 3 71
Suffeth Davis Jun 16 86
Vachal Davis May 22 65; Aug 21 66;
     Mar 27 70; Aug 22 71
William Davis May 8 65; n.d.
Francis Davis, Junr Jun 26 71
William Davis, Junr May 12 67;
     Dec 14 68
George Dawson Jun 17 67
Moses Deaslin Jan 26 71
John Delander May 16 69
John Delauder Feb 27 73
Laurence Delonder Apr 16 71
William Denis Nov 17 66
John Depue Aug 19 66
Casper Devilbess Apr 22 71
Serrat Dickenson Jul 9 71
Thomas Dickison May 9 69
Richardson Donaldson Jul 3 66
Basil Dorsey Jun 12 73
Michael Dottro Apr 5 70
James Douley, Junr Apr 18 71
Rachel Dowden Nov 27 74
Richard Dowden Sep 28 65
Peter Dowell Oct 15 70
Joseph Draik Oct 9 71
Thomas Duly Nov 28 70
Conrod Dutton Jul 20 69
Alexander Duvall Jun 5 69; Jul 6 69
Lewis Duvall May 3 65; Sep 8, 75
Lewis Duvall, son of Benjamin
     Jul 30 65
William Duvall May 27 66
Harmon Eagle Sep 30 72
John Eason Jun 14 69
George Easter 24 1765
John Easton Jan 6 68
Christian Eaverhart Apr 28 73
Robert Edes Dec 12 70
Frederick Eison Dec 12 68; Jun 13 68
William Elerburten Jun 24 65
Mark Ellett May 14 67
Samuel Ellis Aug 15 67
Zachariah Ellis Jun 26 72
Zachariah Ellis, living about 5 miles
     below the mouth of the Monococy
     Jun 11 71

William England Jan 14 68
Philip Ensmuger May 24 70
Adam Estor Aug 8 67
Edward Evans Jan 5 75
Joseph Evans, near the great Falls,
    Potomack Apr 23 66
Joseph Everit, living near Little
    Pipe Mar 19 73
Baltis Fait Jan 24 74
Samuel Farmer Nov 3 73
Moses Farquhar May 15 75
William Farquhar Sep 1 72
Barnett Faud Aug 30 75
John Ferguson, living between two
    Pipe Creeks Jun 12 73
Mathias Fickle living near Tawney
    Town Jul 28 74; Aug 2 74
Adam Fisher Sep 24 65
Martin Fisher Dec 6 69
Henry Fister Jul 7 70
James Fleming Aug 30 73
Samuel Fleming Aug 5 66
John Fletchall May 16 69; May 21 71
William Flinthem Mar 27 67
Robert Flora Jun 2 68
Ann Foard, living on Rock Creek, 9
    miles from Geo. Town Jan 22 73
Philip Fogel Dec 4 65
Andrew Fogle Jul 27 72
John Ford Feb 4 66
Peter Ford Sep 20 65
Henary Fore Feb 8 70
John Forman Jun 17 65
Jacob Foute Sep 9 67
William Fracey, Junr Jan 2 69
Frederick Fraise Apr 5 65; Jun 19 66
Michael Frank May 12 66
Joseph Franklin Jul 18 75
Henry Frazier Jun 19 75
Jacob French Mar 8 70
Thomas French Dec 5 70; Feb 14 71
Andrew Frey Jul 24 67
Michael Fundalin, near Taney Town Aug
    11 72
Michael Funk Mar 20 66
James Fyfe Jul 24 66
James Fyfe, living on Seneca near the
    Sugarlands Apr 20 69
Basil Gaither Jun 17 67; Mar 21 72;
    Oct 7 72
Edward Gaither son of Benjamin May 21
    70

Henry Gaither Jun 21 68
Mony Galford Jun 17 65
John Gallaway Mar 28 70
James Galt May 27 69
Benjamin Galton May 14 64; Jun 17 67
Richard Gatton Apr 8 67
Albright George Dec 28 69
Ashmon Ginkings Jan 8 65
Ashmon Ginkins May 15 66
Samuel Glaze Oct 17 70
Humphrey Godman Jun 28 74; May 27 75
William Goforth Jul 4 69
William Good Jul 30 66
Benjamin Goodrick Jun 22 71
Alexander Grant Dec 6 65; Aug 7 70
Thomas Graves Sep 17 71
Thomas Graves, living on the road
    near Georgetown Oct 2 66
William Graves Jun 26 71
John Gray Aug 8 70
John Gray, living on tract called
    Pourk(?) Hall, on Little Pipe
    Creek Jun 14 70
Thomas Green May 15 66
William Green Sep 19 65
Charles Greenbury Griffith May 5 74
Walter Smith Greenfield May 22 65
William Grey Mar 10 68
Jacob Gripe, Junr Aug 11 68
Abraham Haff Jun 27 67; May 9 71;
    Jun 29 72; Apr 5 73; Apr 21 75;
    Oct 9 75
Richard Haff Apr 29 73; Sep 20 73
Jonathan Hager Sep 18 65; Apr 24 67
Benjamin Hall of Burnt Housewood
    Hundred Jul 27 65
Benjamin Hall, Junr Jul 4 68
Michael Hall Apr 22 71
Ralph Halt Jun 13 69
John Hamel Dec 22
Francis Hamilton Aug 16 72
William Hanker Apr 30 65
Samuel Hanson May 29 72
William Harbert Nov 8 70
Samuel Hardesty Jul 19 71
John Hardin, Junr Jun 8 68
Charles Harding May 6 71
Francis Hardister Jul 12 69
Conrod Hargawder Nov 16 72
William Harison, near the widdow
    Hobbs Jul 6 65

Isaac Harlan Sep 8 66
Jacob Harman May 31 75
Josiah Harper Sep 2 66
Josiah Harper, near Harpers ferry Apr
 15 65
Aaron Harris May 22 74
William Harris Oct 21 66
Michael Hartman Nov 30 67
Henry Hartsock, living near Conrod
 Dottros Dec 7 71
Henry Hawk Aug 29 68
William Hawker May 20 72
John Hawkings Apr 19 68
Thomas Hawkings Jun 21 68
John Hawkins Aug 16 75
William Hays Aug 16 68; Aug 24 70
Jeremiah Hayse Jul 7 68
William Edward Head Aug 24 71
William Head, Junr Apr 8 69
Michael Heavly Nov 14 75
Joseph Helm Aug 21 66
Hendrick Hendrickson Sep 30 68
John Hennongirth Jul 30 65
Fortnoy Henry Aug 23 73
Marks Hermon Mar 8 66
Mathious Herschman Dec 3 67
Joshua Hervin Jul 21 69
Jacob Hess Feb 23 70
Michael Heyler Feb 17 74
David Hickman Feb 2 69
David Hickman, living in the
 Sugarland May 9 69
Margaret Hickman, living about 10
 miles below mouth of Monococy May
 8 71
John Higgins Jul 5 74
Abm. Hill Mar 30 75
Isaac Hill Jun 16 71
James Hill Jan 25 74
Ralff Crab Hilleary Dec 8 66
Andrew Hime Jun 4 71
Ballsor Hinkle Jun 8 74
Thomas Hinton Jun 19 67; May 19 70;
 Jun 14 74
Adam Hisung Aug 16 75
Joseph Hobbs Feb 29 67
Joseph Hobbs and Nathan Magruder Apr
 12 75
Nicholas Hobbs Oct 2 72
Josua Hobs May 21 73
Capewell Holland, Junr Mar 24 69
Anthony Holmead Aug 23 65

Frederick Holtshoble Nov 16 68
Henry Hoover, near Shockeys Gap Jul
 24 75
Jacob Hoover Nov 11 75
Andrew House Mar 15 68
George House Jun 18 66
Isaac Houser Jan 26 70
Robert Houstie Nov 12 71
Paul Hoy(e) Aug 18 73; May 9 74
Henry Huffman Aug 30 70
Rudolph Huffman Feb 15 66
James Hughs Aug 2 73
John Hughs Jun 16 69; Jun 16 73
Jacob Human Jul 24 73
Jacob Hummer Jun 7 66
Peter Ingle, farmer, Jul 11 75
William Ingram Aug 23 69
Jeremiah Jack Aug 15 74; Jun 20 75
John Jackson Jun 19 75
Elizabeth Jacobs Jul 12 71; Jul 8 74;
 May 13 75
John Jacobs Jun 30 66
Grifey James Dec 24 74
Joseph Jean, overseer of John Chisolm
 Jan 6 66
William Jeans Mar 22 67
Thomas Jennings, Esqr. Aug 21 66
John Jerdon Apr 7 70
John Jessper Nov 29 69
Thomas Johnson, Junr Mar 14 72
Josiah Jones May 16 69
Peter Jones Mar 22 67
Thomas Jones Nov 5 68
Mosis Juel Mar 24 70
William Juel Nov 1 68
Isaac Julin Sep 7 71
Conrad Kareas, living near head of
 Linganore & Sams Creek Nov 7 67
Adam Karr, living near Christian
 Koonces Nov 2 71
Conrod Katuldy Mar 22 75
Peter Keephart May 9 67
John Keeser May 27 74
William Keley Jan 9 75
Julana Kellor Sep 1 74
Samuel Kelly May 2 67; Jul 7 68
Peter Kemp Nov 28 67
Martin Keplinger Apr 3 69
John Keysinger May 31 67
John George Kidaman Jul 4 70
John Kincer Apr 17 71
Richard King Aug 10 72

George Kirk Jun 16 72; Jun 8 73
Thomas Kirk, Junr May 10 69
Jacob Klein Dec 29 71
Nickolus Kline Aug 5 69
Thomas Knotts Aug 17 69
Mathew Laney Jan 20 69
John Larain, living near the mouth of
    Manocacy May 21 73
George William Laurance Aug 6 66
Mary Lawrance Jan 17 70
Thomas Laysur Nov 5 68
Henry Lazenby Jul 14 67
Jacob Lear Oct 12 71
Godfrey Leatherman Nov 22 68
Henry Leatherman Aug 6 70
Nicholas Leatherman Jan 27 69
Peter Lebegh Oct 23 72
Aaron Lee Jun 9 67
Robert Lee Nov 4 69
Jacob Leece Sep 11 70; Oct 25 73
Robert Lemar Dec 6 71
Aaron Lenham Aug 20 71
Zachariah Lenthicum Oct 26 74
Henry Letherman Sep 2 73; Oct 30 73
Michael Letton Apr 17 70
Henry Levens Aug 25 72
Jonathan Lewis Dec 12 70
Adam Lighty Jun 20 67
James Lingo Sep 15 68
Andrew Link Jul 24 67
Joseph Linthicom Sep 6 65; Oct 14 67
Samuel Linton Jun 8 74
Michael Litton Apr 3 65
Andrew Livingston Jul 13 73
John Livingston May 7 66
Michael Lofter May 16 74
James Logen Aug 6 66
Matthias Long, living near Smiths
    Mill, upon Pipe Creek Jul 25 68
William Luckett Jun 27 67; Mar 9 68
William Luckett, Junr May 27 65;
    Mar 28 69
Moses Luman Aug 18 75
Mary Lydy Aug 24 71
Thomas Maccubbin May 28 70
John Macginnis Nov 14 67
Benjamin Mackall Feb 12 66
James Mackatee Aug 9 73
James Mackey Apr 19 75; Jul 28 75
John Madam Sep 2 68
Mordecai Madden Nov 11 71
Alexander Magruder May 17 66

Mary Magruder Jul 28 65
Nathan Magruder with Joseph Hobbs Apr
    12 75
Ninean Beall Magruder Jul 21 66
William Beall Magruder Jun 10 71
James Makall May 22 75
William Manford Dec 18 67
George Mann Dec 15 74
James Manningore Jun 24 65
James Mantz Mar 29 75
John Marker Aug 4 75
Matthias Mart, living near Paul
    Woolfs near Little Creek Jul 24 69
John Mason Sep 28 65; Aug 30 68
Jacob May Sep 12 66; Jun 21 68
James McBride Mar 15 69
James McCay Jun 27 67
James McClain Aug 31 65
William McClellan Jun 22 56
Daniel McCoy Aug 2 70
James McCoy Nov 29 72
Joseph McDonald May 29 73
William McGaughey Aug 15 66
John McGinnes Nov 28 69
Peter McMullen Sep 28 67
Robert McNutt Jun 22 68
John Meal Dec 15 69
Joseph Mershon Nov 5 74
John Meyer Apr 2 66
John Mifford, living near Paul
    Woolf's Tavern May 26 71
Daniel Miller Aug 12 72
David Miller Aug 12 71; Sep 14 71;
    Sep 25 75
Isaac Miller Aug 8 70
Isaac Miller, Fishing Creek Sep 26 65
Jacob Miller Dec 7 67
Jacob Miller of Kittocton Dec 31 71
Michael Miller Sep 8 65
Thomas Miller Nov 7 67
John Mitter May 27 69
Phillipseany Moarner Mar 11 74
John Moore Jul 25 68
Felix Morgan Jul 19 70
Richard Morgan Dec 15 70
William Morris Jul 1 75
Jarvis Moss Jan 9 75
Thomas Mounts Dec 5 69; Jun 4 71
Luke(r) Mudd Aug 5 67; Jul 9 69;
    Jul 16 71; May 26 73
Charles Murphy Oct 21 71; Mar 18 72
John Musgrove Jan 1 71

Samuel Musgrove Mar 11 74
Peter Musser Jan 23 73
Henry Myers, living near Ludowick
    Yost Jul 7 70
Conrod Myre, living about 10 miles
    below mouth of Monocacy Oct 26 73
Nathan Nabors Jul 15 66
Thomas Narrison Nov 28 74
Rudy Naughtinger Nov 21 71
George Nead, living near mouth of
    Pipe Creek Apr 22 71
Jacob Neaff, Junr Oct 16 69
George Need Jun 1 67
Doctr. Charles Neel Jul 18 68
Benjamin Nicholls Nov 7 73
Thomas Nicholls Jan 7 73
Thomas Nicholls, Junr Jun 13 71
James Nicholls, near the Lower Falls
    Nov 28 72
Beckett Nichols Sep 4 74
William Nicholson Oct 17 72
John Nickols Feb 27 70
Jonathan Nixon Aug 7 70
Sampson Noland Jun 16 69
Sampson Noland, living about 8 miles
    below mouth of Monococy Apr 5 71
Thomas Noland May 12 72; May 17 74
Joseph Norris May 5 70; Oct 29 71
William Seir Norris Mar 4 66
Benjamin Norris, Junr May 25 69
Benjamin Norriss, Senr Aug 3 67
Richard Northcraft Jan 2 72
Richard Norwood May 2 65
Michael Null, Senr Sep 8 66
Michael O'Donnall Dec 8 72
John Odaniel Oct 14 75
David John Oden Oct 23 70
James Offutt Jun 10 71
Mrs. Sarah Offutt Aug 24 69
Nathaniel Offutt May 12 72
Thomas Offutt Dec 14 68; Mar 20 71;
    May 18 71
Benjamin Ogle Aug 6 67
Joseph Ogle, living at mouth of Toms
    Creek May 14 68
Thomas Ogle Feb 14 69
Christopher Ohaven Jul 22 65
William Oneal Oct 25 66
Jeremiah Orme, living near Walter
    Beall's Mill Jun 3 71
Moses Orme Jun 2 73
Christian Orndorff Jun 21 68

Henry Orndorff Oct 15 67
Mathias Otto Aug 25 67
John Owen Mar 23 71
Robert Owen May 21 70
Sarah Owen Jan 10 68
Rachael Owings Mar 6 71
Samuel Owings Nov 19 66
Rachel Owins Aug 6 66
Flayll Pain Dec 29 67
Frail Pain Apr 6 65; Aug 10 68
John Pain Aug 28 67
Gideon Palmer Aug 8 67
James Paradice Nov 1 69
Jeremiah Patrick Jun 28 66
John Patterson Oct 30 66
George Peack May 4 68
Jacob Peckelshimer May 27 72
Sarah Pedecord Sep 1 67
William Pedecord Sep 5 67
Harrison Pelley Apr 23 66
William Perkabile Sep 22 66
Samuel Perle Feb 1 71
Samuel Perry May 3 71
Robert Peter Oct 17 72
Thomas Pettey Aug 1 67
John Philips Apr 1 75
Nicholous Phillips Jun 17 65
Leonard Pickenpaugh Apr 10 71
Peter Pickingpaw Sep 3 70
James Piels Dec 14 68
Clement Pierce May 17 73
John Pigman Jun 26 71
Nathaniel Pigman Aug 3 71
James Piles May 9 68
Thomas Pindall Aug 15 69
Peter Pinkley May 22 65; Aug 25 67
Joseph Piper Aug 24 68
Joseph Plumer Jun 26 65
George Plummer May 3 66; May 1 71;
    Mar 18 73
John Plummer Nov 14 72
Philamon Plummer Apr 21 68; Nov 14 72
Thomas Plummer son of Samuel
    Jul 15 73
Joseph Pool, living about 2 miles
    from Monococy Chapel May 3 70
Henry Poole Jul 5 75
Phillip Porter, near Sarah Hobbs
    (Fred Co) Oct 27 66
John Pottenger Jun 17 65
Richard Powel Jun 4 68
Thomas Powell Sep 24 67; Oct 10 75

John Power Jun 14 71
Laurence Prangle Aug 31 71
Thomas Price, at the head of Bennet's
    Creek Nov 14 72
Henry Priest May 14 67
Joseph Prigmore Nov 17 66
James Prosser Mar 8 68
Henry Prout Oct 13 70
John Quadrent Aug 9 66
John Raitt Jul 13 72
Jacob Ramsberg May 21 73
Michael Rape (Ratie?) Mar 21 70
John Rawlings May 16 68
Andrew Redrug May 9 74
Samuel Reed Aug 21 65
Andrew Rentch Sep 5 68
John Reyley May 22 72
Joseph Reynolds Jul 23 70
Thomas Reynolds May 23 65
Christian Rhorar Mar 2 66
John Rhorar Mar 3 66
Samuel Rhorar Jan 8 73
John Rhorrar Apr 26 69
Christian Rhorrer Feb 23 68
George Rice Aug 7 68
Daniel Richards Jul 8 71
Arabella Richardson Sep 5 73
Thomas Richardson Mar 19 65;
    Jun 1 71
Isaac Richey Jun 6 68
Thomas Richford Jun 29 70
Anthony Rickets Jun 16 67
Adam Ridenower Jan 3 1770
Henry Ridenour Aug 16 70
Thomas Rider Dec 8 67
Richard Ridgely Dec 14 75
Joseph Ridgeway Jun 22 71
Jacob Ridenour Feb 20 75
John Riggs Sep 8 70
Philip Rimel Dec 3 65
Mathias Ringer Oct 12 67; May 13 71;
    Sep 6 75
Samuel Roarer Jul 30 73
William Robason Jul 27 73
William Roberts Aug 12 72
James Robinson Jun 26 69
Christian Rode May 25 65
Jacob Rode or Road Aug 26 68
Philip Rodebeler Aug 5 73
Phillip Rodenbiller May 6 65
Philip Rodenpeler Jun 18 72
Lodowick Roderick Jul 4 74

Andrew Roderock Apr 5 65
Michael Roof Nov 17 73
Jacob Rossell Aug 19 66
Daniel Rudey Aug 11 68
James Rugles Dec 7 67
Michael Runer Jul 17 73
John Saffell Jul 1 75
Abraham Sagkim Apr 9 66
William Sander, living on Potomack
    below the mouth of Monocacy,
    May 26 69
George Saxton Jul 23 73
James Scot Jan 18 75
John Scott Aug 22 71
Thomas Scott Aug 20 71
Peter Seddy Jul 24 67
James Sergent May 31 73
Sarah Shall (Shaw?) Apr 19 74
Christian Sheaver, living near West
    Minister Town May 24 72
Sarah Shepherd Jul 21 65
Simon Shever Aug 5 68
John Shilling May 10 75
Henry Shneboly Jun 10 73
Christopher Shockey May 31 65
George Shour May 22 71
Peter Shover Jul 31 75
Christian Shryock May 22 71
Daniel Shults Aug 23 66; Jul 21 67
Samuel Shurts Sep 17 72
Jacob Sigler Apr 21 73
Philip Silor Oct 17 68
John Silvers Jun 12 73
Samuel Simons May 10 69
John Simpson Oct 11 74
Philip Sinn May 29 72
Sabra Siscel Apr 15 72
Richard Skaggs Junr Apr 16 72;
    Jan 11 75
Walter Skiner Jan 8 66
Richard Skuggs Jun 22 73
Daniel Smith Oct 9 70
Jacob Smith Jan 2 72
James Smith Dec 6 69
Middleton Smith May 2 67
Phillip Smith Jan 5 67; May 22 71
Robert Smith Sep 6 66
Thomas Spalding Jul 8 74
Richard Speak Aug 12 72
William Speake Nov 1 69
Jeriniall Spiers Feb 9 69
Jeremiah Spires Nov 16 72

Benjamin Spycher Aug 17 74
Jacob Staley May 4 75
Jacob Stallings Jan 14 75
Joseph Stallion Feb 14 66
Dinel Stephenson Aug 16 72
Thomas Steuart May 17 66
Henry Stoner Nov 23 71
George Stricker Jun 3 71; Jun 15 72;
    Jun 7 73
Michael Stricker Jun 4 71; Nov 18 75
Killeon Strider Apr 20 75
Michael Striker Jun 6 74
Christopher Stull Jun 16 71
Valentine Sumer Jul 31 69
Felty Summers May 18 65
Edward Swainy May 27 65; May 11 73
Andrew Swan Jun 6 75
Charles Swearingem Aug 16 69
Van Swearingem Jr. Jun 29 73
Samuel Swearingen Jul 24 69
Van Swearingen Jul 2 74
Mary Swinford Jun 18 66
Melchor Tabler May 27 71; May 6 74
William Talbott Jul 7 66; Aug 10 67;
    May 18 71
John Tanehill Nov 13 71
Ninian Tannehill Jun 12 71
Ninian Tawnihill Aug 16 68
John Teem Aug 21 72
Benjamin Thomas May 18 65
Elizabeth Thomas Aug 31 71
Jonathan Thomas Oct 2 69
Rebecca Thomas Jul 27 74
Richard Thrall Jul 9 70
Jesse Tomlinson, living near Elias
    Delashmutt, Junr - Sep 5 70
Henry Toms Apr 5 65
Robert Toon Sep 19 67
John Trammel Jun 10 71
Adam Troup Mar 7 74
Adom Troup Dec 19 74
Michael Troutman May 17 66; Aug 28
    67; May 25 70
Christian Troxell Dec 27 66;
    May 27 67; Jul 26 68
Ann Trundel, widdow, living near
    Walter Beall's mill - Apr 15 71
Josiah Trundell Apr 29 73
John Trundle Aug 17 68
Thomas Trunnel Sep 9 77
Goodheart Trussels Jul 28 67
Jonathan Tucker Jun 15 71; May 12 74

William Tucker Aug 10 70; Jul 31 71
Charles Turner Apr 7 68
William Turner of Linganore May 6 65
Casper Turst(?) Apr 23 72
Michael Tutaror, Junr Sep 8 66
Nicholas Umstid, living near Sams
    Creek Jun 9 69
Unckle Unckles of Pipe Creek
    Jul 8 66
Henry Unsell Dec 17 66
John Veatch May 2 66
Nathan Veatch Jul 10 71
Daniel Vince, living near mouth of
    Linganore Jul 6 70
Daniel Vines May 10 73
Charles Walker Jun 27 65; Jun 11 66;
    Oct 22 67
Michael Walker Jan 13 65
Zephaniah Walker Apr 26 69
Francis Wallace May 26 68; Jan 18 71
William Wallace Mar 10 69
James Wallace, Senr Jun 19 66
Thomas Waller, Junr Sep 30 66
Daniel Walter May 23 65
George Walter, living in the
    Sugarlands - Jun 21 69
Jacob Walter May 18 65
John Walter Jul 27 67
Josephus Walters Aug 11 73
Joseph Warford Apr 19 65
Jacob Warnfields Apr 28 75
Samuel Warters Mar 20 70
Richard Waters Jun 3 69
Thomas Waters Apr 5 65
John Watson, near Rock Creek
    Jul 14 66
Richard Watts Aug 3 65
Richard Watts, living near Mr.
    (Mrs.?) Dowden Jun 20 69
Peter Wayrey Jun 4 74
Peter Wayrey(?) Oct 4 69
John Weavour Dec 7 74
John Web Apr 26 75
Peter Weddel Aug 1 70
Thomas Welch Jul 12 70
Jacob Weller, Junr Aug 11 66
Thomas Wells Feb 6 67; May 7 73
John West son of William Jun 17 67
Joseph West Sr. May 4 74
Joseph West, Junr, recorded his mark
    Oct 2 66
David White Jul 28 72

John White Aug 27 67
Joseph White Jun 16 67
Joseph White, living near the Lower
    Falls - Aug 6 70
Leonard White Jun 24 70
John Whitmore May 14 70; Jul 31 72
Charles Williams Apr 20 74
Francis Williams Jan 20 74
Henry Williams Jun 10 75
John Willson Jan 6 66
Josiah Willson Jun 28 74
Sadworth Willson, living about 5
    miles below mouth of Monococy
    Dec 28 69
Thomas Willson Jan 28 67
William Willson Jun 27 72
Henry Wilson May 15 71
Isaac Wilson Jul 4 71
Thomas Wilson May 7 71
Wadsworth Wilson Nov 16 73
Walter Wilson Mar 19 73
Thomas Winder Jan 14 74
Francis Winrod Nov 20 73
Peter Winrode Jun 20 72
Ignatious Winser Jan 13 68
Mary Winsor Jun 22 69
George Winter Oct 5 69
Benjamin Witmore Sep 12 69
Paul Wolf May 11 69
Conrod Wolford Jun 6 74
Charles Wood Apr 27 65
John Wood Sep 14 65; Jun 11 74
Robert Wood May 22 75
Thomas Wood, living near where Collo.
    Samuel Beall lived - Nov 3 70
Francis Woodward living near Rock
    Creek Church May 23 74
Paul Woolf Sep 2 68
Conrad Woolfkill Nov 13 75
Thomas Sprigg Wotton Jun 18 66
Amos Wright Nov 21 70
Harman Yoot Jul 9 74
James Young Jun 7 68
Lodowick Young Nov 8 75
Daniel Zacharias Nov 20 65

Rent Due on land in Frederick County, 1768-1769

A list of persons who stand charged with lands on Frederick county Rent
Rolls which are under such circumstances as renders it out of the power of
George Scott Farmer afsaid County to Collect the Rents, and therefore claims
allowance under his articles for the same from March(?) 1768 to March(?)
1769

Alexander Adams, himself and land in
    Pa
John Adamson
Ann Agnew
Christian Allbaugh
Eve Allbaugh
William Allerburton
William Almary
William Anderson
Daniel Arshcraft's heirs unknown
Samuel Agnew
William Alldreidge all uncultivated
    and himself no constant place of
    abode and will not pay
Thomas Awbrey, lives in Virginia

Alexander Bailey
Abram Baker
Peter Baker, says is charged to Saml
    Baker
James Baldwin
Daniel Baldwin living in Pa
Jacob Ballsell
Richard Barnes
Thomas Bassett, lives in Pa
Thomas Bassett, Phila (addl)
David Beagler
Mark Beagler
Captain Alexander Beall's heirs
Archibald Beall
Edward Beall
George Beall Junr
James Beall of Ninian
John Beall of Robert
--hn Beall's heirs
Benjamin Beall's heirs
William Beall's heirs
William Beall of Ninian
Thomas Beane, lives in PG Co
Jacob Bearur, lives in Pa
James Beatty
Susanah Beatty, is dead and they who
    own the land say she owned no more
    than 81 1/2 and will pay no more
Benjamin Becraft
Mary Belt

Joseph Bennett
Thomas Bentley, gone to Carolina
Jacob Bishop
---m Black, in England
John Bob
Andrew Booker
Peter Booker
John Boone, 1 lot in Geo. Town
William Boyd
Solmon Brewer
James Brooke's heirs
James Brooke (addl)
Lucey Brooke
Mary Brookes
Henry Brothers, lives in Pa
Benjamin Brown, gone to Carolinas
David Brown himself and land in Pa
William Brown, he and land in Pa
John Brown of Joshua
Edward Browns
Peter Bruner
John Bukurduke Ball, Balt Co
Everhart Bumgardner
Richard Bumgardner
Yost Bunkle
Elizabeth Burcham, Va
Matheas Burkett's heirs
George Burnes
William Burnes, lives in Va
Tobias Butler
Peter Butler's heirs
Henry Byer

Philip Caffee, dead
John Campbell
John Carr
William Chadd, a stroler
William Chapline
Henry Charlton, lives in Pa
Saml Chase
Zachariah Cheany
Greenbury Cheany, dead
Josiah Claphan, lives in Va
George Clark
Thomas Clarkson

Johny Clary
William Clary
William Deveron(?) Clary
Tiel Clements
John Cochran, him and land in Pa
William Cochran, himself and land in
 Pa
John Colwell's heirs, Va
Thomas Conn, gone to Carolina
Devall Coonce
George Coonce, Pa or Balt Co
Frederick Cooper
Nicholas Corben
John Cowman
Henry Wright Crabb's heirs
John Crawford, him and land in Pa
Michael Creagar senr
Jacob Creasy, is dead
--- Crise
William Cumming's heirs

George Dagan
Henry Darbey
Ann Davis
David Davis
Meredith Davis's heirs
Wm. Davis's heirs
Phenehas Davis, lives in Pa
Sarah & Mary Davis; Sarah is in AA Co
Thomas Davison, Pa
Leonard Decaes, dead
James Decker
James Dickson's heirs
Edward Diggis and Ralph Taney
John Diggis's heirs
Henry Diggis, lives in Pa
Captain John Dorsey's heirs
Basil Dorsey's heirs
John Dorsey's heirs
The Honble D. Dulany Esq.
Samuel Dullenbaugh
John Dunn's heirs unknown
Christian Dyer

George Easter
William Eastub
Ninian Edmonston
Ulerick Ekler
John Emmetts
John England
Joseph Ensor
Adam Erchard

Walter Evans, in PG Co
John Everet, lives in Pa

Henry Fight, lives in Balt Co
Peter Fine, lives out of the Province
John Flint, is dead; his son the heir
 lives in Va
Simon Foy
Nicholas France
Jason Frizzle, gone to Carolina

Richard Gabriel, himself and land in
 Pa
Benjamin Gaither, in AA Co or Balt Co
Fielder Gantt (addl)
John Gardner
Isaac Garrison
Jacob Giles - belongs to Jos. Waters
 a stroler
Thomas Gilliland's heirs
Josiah Gordon, PG Co
George Gordon's heirs
George Graff
Philip Grambler
Jacob Grams
Benjamin Griffith, AA Co
Orlander Griffith, AA Co
John Gronon
Joseph Groves
Fielder Gantt

Jonathan Hagan
Henry Hall, is dead
Shadrech Harmon
George Hartman
George Frazier Hawkins
Margaret Hern, both her and land
 suppd in Pa
Patrick Hinds (addl)
John Howard, Carolina
John Hyer
John Larkins
Valentine Larsh
James Lemar, gone to Carolina
Saml Lewellin, Pa
Charls Lewis
Philip Litzinger, Va
Jonas Luby
Wm. Lucas

Alexander Magruder
John Magruder

Nathaniel Magruder
Ninian Magruder
Samuel Magruder
Paul Mark's heirs
Edmond Martin
James Martin
Joseph Hardman's heirs
Martin Hilderbrand
George Matthews
Rowland May
William McClary, all in Pa
William McCrachan, Va
William McCray
Moses McCubbin, Balt Co
Wm. McGaughy a stroler
Thomas McHaine
John McIntire
Thomas McKeene both him and land in
    Pa
Saml McKeene himself and land in Pa
Thomas McLane
William McLane
Patrick McManning
Alexander McNear
Honesty Medley
Conrod Miller
Isaac Miller
John Miller
Lodwick Miller
Oliver Miller, Balt Co (addl)
Thomas Miller
Michael Miller heirs
Jacob Miller Jr
Oliver Miller, Balt Co
Morris Millhouses heirs, part lies in
    Pen
George Valeninte Milsgars
Isaac Milton's heirs
Mary Anne Mislin
John Mitchel, a minor in Chas Co
David Mitchell
Thomas Morris
Samuel Mount, Va
Thomas Mullineux, Balt Co
Philip Murphy's heirs

George Neale
Raphael Neale, St. Marys Co
Benjamin Nearson
George Neat
Mathias Need
Christian New

Jacob Nicholls
Samuel Nicholls
Thomas Nicholls
Thomas Nicholls' heirs
John Nichols, in AA Co
Benjamin Nickring
Thomas Noble's heirs
William Norris's heirs
Andrew Nubinger
Jacob Null

Nathaniel Offutt Junr
Major Joseph Ogle's heirs
Thomas Orbison, lives in Pen
Joshua Owen, Balt Co
Samuel Owings Junr

William Paca
George Pack's heirs
Thomas Palmer, in Pa
Richard Pernall
James Perry, PG Co
Elias Pettitt - runaway
Nicholas Philips, Va
Thomas Philpot, London
Thomas Pickerton
Jacob Piper
Thomas Claget Prather's heirs, gone
    to Red Stone
Peter Praig
Samuel Price
William Price of Rheese Run
Casper Primore
John Radford's heirs
John Ralston, himself and land in Pa
William Raven
John Ray, AA Co
Valentine Reap
John Reddick, Balt Co, land in Pa
Andrew Reed
Frederick Reel
John Richards
John Ridgeley, Balt Co
Mary Ridgeway
Elisha Riggs
Jeremiah Riley
John Riley
Aaron Riley, belongs to a merchant in
    Phila
Peter Ritcher
William Rivert, said to live in Pa
Stephen Robert

Lawrance Rombarah
Doctor David Ross
John Row, dead
William Rugdon, both himself and land
   in Pa
John Ruister, Balt Co
William Rusk, himself and land in Pa
Thomas Rutland, AA Co

Nicholas Samuel
John Sausar, is run away
William Scott, lives in Va
Andrew Scott's heirs
James Sears dead
John Sharra
Captain Evan Shelbey
David Shelbey, lives in Pa
Jacob Shilling
William Shoup, Va
John Shudey
Isaac Simmons
John Simple, lives in Va
Andrew Simpson
John Sittern's heirs
Richard Skith
George Slator
George Sloy
George Smith
Jacob Smith, a stroler
John Smiths heirs
Frederick Sower
William Spartis
Conrad Spaw
Leonard Spong
Joseph Sprigg, PG Co
Captain Edward Spriggs
Gilbert Sprigg's heirs
Osburn Sprigg's heirs
Colo Edward Sprigg's heirs (the widow
   pays for 593 acres)
James Spurgeon
John Spurgeon
James Spurgeon, both him and land in
   Pa (addl)
Benjamin Spyker
Tobias Stansbury's heirs
William Starr, gone to Carolina
James Stephenson, both him and land
   in Pa
William Stewart, Pa
Thomas Stoddert's heirs
Henry Stolae

Henry Stone
William Stroope, Va
Jacob Sunfrang
Edward Swaney
Benedict Swope (addl)
Benedict Swope, Balt Co
Aexander and Andrew Symmers
Thomas Tallbert
Ralph Taney with Edward Diggis
George Tayler
Anthony Thompson
Cornelius and Ann Thompson
John Thompson dead
Captain Wm. Tipple
Edward Totheral, lives in England
Caleb Touchstone
Sampson Trammell, Va
Widow Tranceway
Jacob Trout
John Trundle
Frrederick Tryor
Edmond Turner, PG Co

Frederick Unsell

John Vammons, Pen, both him and land
James Verdie
Jeremiah Virgin

Hance Waggoner, gone to Carolina
George Wales
William Wallace's heirs
Edward Ward
Basil Warfield, Eastern Shore
Joseph Warford, both him and land in
   Pa
William Warford, Carolina
James Warford, gone to Carolina
Joseph Waters a stroler
Nathan Waters, AA Co
William Waters, in gone
John Watts, both him and land in Pa
William Waugh's heirs
John Weaver
John Webster, AA Co
Alexander Wells, Balt Co
Thomas Wells, Balt Co
Stephen West
William West's heirs
Nathaniel Wickham senr
William Wilkins
Thomas Willet

Rent Due on land in Frederick County, 1768-1769

John Williams
Eleanor Williams, in Pa
Esther Williams, in Pa
Gerard Willson
John Willson, PG Co
Thomas Willson

William Willson Greenwood
John Wilmot Junr, AA Co
Francis Wise's heirs
Jane Wivell
John Woolf
John Worthington Junr, Balt Co

Rent Due on Land in Frederick County, 1771-1772

A List of Persons who stand charged with lands on Fredk Co which are under such circumstances as rendered it out of the Power of George ... Farmer of the said County to collect the Rents and therefore Claims Allowance under his articles for the same - from Michael mass 1771 to Michael mass 1772

Thos. Abrey, lives in Va
Mark Alexander and Andw Stigar, they
    live in Balt Co
Christian Allbaugh
Eve Allbaugh
John Alldridge (addl)
William Alldridge a single man and no
    place of abode
William Allerberton's heirs
William Allmary
Daniel Ashcrafts heirs
James Baldwin, lives in PG Co
Jacob Banker
Jacob Barnes
Richard Barnes
Thos. Bassett, lives in Pa
Alexander Bayley
Michael Beagler
William Murdock Beall
Robt Beall (of Jas) (addl)
John Beall of Robt heirs
Capt Alexr Beall's heirs
John Beall's heirs
William Beall's heirs
William Beall's heirs, this land
    belongs to minors
Patrick Beall, lives in PG Co
Edward Beall, no constant place of
    abode
John Beane
Richard Beard, man and land in Pa
Chas. Beatty
William Beatty
Chas. Beatty & Geo Fraser Hawkins,
    lots in Geo. Town

Susannah Beatty, she is dead
Mary Belt (wife of Col. Jeremiah),
    she lives in PG Co
Benjamin Belt Junr; lives in PG Co
Col. Joseph Belt's heirs, lives in PG
    Co
Thos. Belt; lives in PG Co
William Thos. Benson
Thos. Bentley
--- Best
John Bishop, lives in Pa
Samuel Biusey
William Black, lives in London
Brice Blair
Allen Bowie; he lives in PG Co
John Bowman
David Bowser
Abram Boyd's Children, minors
Robert Brightwell's heirs
--- Brooke's heirs
Henry Brothers, lives in Pa
Benjamin Brown
Edward Brown
James Brumlee, lives in Pa
William Buchanan
John Buckerduke
Elizabeth Burcham
Jehew Burkhart
Richard Butler
Peter Butler's heirs
Philip Butman
Henry Byer
Patrick Caile
Messrs Benedict Calvert & Compy
Neil Campble, a poor man, no effects
John Campble, lives in AA Co
John Carehart (addl)
John Carmack

Chas. Carroll Esqr
Jacob Carsner
William Chadd, a stroller
Geo. Chairman, lives in Pa
Joseph Chapline
Capt Moses Chapline's heirs
Henry Charlton, lives in Pa
Samuel Chase (addl)
Michael Clapsaddle, a stroller
George Clark
Wm Devorn Clary, runaway
Tule Clements
Philip Coffee
Geo. Coleman
Jacob Coonce
Peter Coonce
Geo. Coonce, lives in Pa
Nicholas Corbin
Henry Wright Crabb's heirs
Mrs. Crabb's heirs
Jacob Crasey, dead, land lies in Pa
Michael Cregar Junr, gone to Va
Stephen Crise
James Cross
Frederick Crouse, lives in Pa
Aron Crusey
John Cuirtain
Joseph Cumberlidge; poor man, no
    effects
Henry Darby
John Darnall; lives in Chas Co
Thomas Davidson, lives in Pa
David Davis, lives in Pa
Isaac Dawson; moved to Red Stone
    Settlement
Francis Deakins (addl)
William Deakins (addl)
Leonard Decoes, man dead
William Dent
Peter Detlinger
James Dickson's heirs
Dudley Diggs, lives in St. Mary's Co
Edward Diggs and Ralph Tawney
Ignatius Diggs
John Diggs' heirs
James Docker
Calib Dorsey
William Downey, a poor man, no
    effects
Richard Duckett and Thos. Williams
Daniel Dulany
Walter Dulany

John Dunn's heirs
William Dunwoody; has gone to Red
    Stone Settlement
John or Samuel Durbin
--- Dyer
Adam Easter
Ninian Edmonston
Rachel Edmonston
Ulerich Eikler
John England
Joseph Ensor, lives in Balt Co
Walter Evans, lives in PG Co
Jacob Eversole
Peter Fine
John Flint Senr, is dead, son lives
    in Va
Charles Allison Foard, lives in
    Charles Co
Edward Fotterall's heirs, heirs in
    Ireland
Jacob French, gone to Va
Benjamin Gaither, lives in AA Co
John Gardner
Isaac Garrison
Thos. Gassaway, lives in AA Co
Fielder Gaunt
William Gibson, no effects on the
    land
Jacob Giles, lives in Balt Co
Mordecai Gist, man gone to the West
    Indies
Geo. Gordon's heirs
Michael Gore, gone to Carolina
Geo. Graff
Francis Grandadam
Thos. Green, gone to Carolina
Orlander Griffith, lives in AA Co
Joseph Groves
Jacob Gunter, lives in Pa
Jonathan Hagar, says char'd to Peter
    Ridenour
William Hall
Charles Hammond (addl)
Nathan Hammond's heirs, heirs live
    in AA Co
Edward Willers Harbine, lives in PG
    Co
William Hardey
Charles Harding
Josiah Harper's heirs, lives in Va
Robert Harper, lives in Va

William Harrison
Robert Harrison, lives in Va
Conrod Hartsog
Nicholas Haslum
Geo. Haun
John Haun
Lodwick Haun
Fredk Wm. Hawker, lives in Va
Geo. Fraser Hawkins, land in Pa
Joseph Hayes
Biggar Head's heirs
Martin Hilderbrand
Thos. Hilleary, lives in PG Co
John Hisler
Peter Hisson, lives in Pa
Hanor Holmes
John Howard, gone to Carolina
Samuel & John Howard, these people
   live in AA Co
Ulerick Huffstadler, lives in Pa
John Hughes
Abram Hull
David Hurley
Thos. Hutchcraft, run away
Samuel Hydes's heirs, he lives in
   England
William Ingleman
John Evan Jenkins
Daniel Jenkins's heirs, belongs to an
   orphan, no effects
John Jessey
Mathew Jones
William Jones
Mountz Justice
John Geo. Keedman
Jacob Kegg, lives in Pa
Charles Kelley
Samuel Kelley, a stroller
Thos. Kellor, lives in Pa
Thos Kennard
John Kennedy's heirs, (minors)
Martin Kersner's heirs
John Keys
William Kimball
Christopher Kitterman, lives in Pa
James Lamar, lives in Carolina
Valentine Larsh, lives in Balt Co
Geo. William Laurance, lives in Va
Patrick Law (addl)
John Layman
Henry Lazenby (addl)
Frederick Leatherman

Philip Ludwell Lee, lives in Va
Geo. Lemmon
Samuel Lewellen, land lays in Pa
Evan Lewis, lives in Pa
John Logsdon (addl)
Laurence Logsdon, gone to Carolina
Ralph Logsdon, is gone to Carolina
John Long
Christopher Lowndes
Jonas Lutz
William Lux, lives in Balt Co
Joseph Lynn
Samuel Lyon, lives at Red Stone
Jonathan Madding
Hezekiah Magruder
Charles Martin
Edmond Martin
John Martin Junr
John Mason, man run away
Leigh Master
Geo. Mathews
Jacob May
Rowland May
William May, a very poor man, no
   effects
Andrew Mayes
William McClary, lands in Pa
William McCray
Capt. Angus McDonald
William McGaughy, lives in Pa
Thos McKain
Hugh McLane
Thos. McLane
Alexander McNear
Honesty Medley
Peter Melattoe
Solomon Miller
Thos. Miller
Isaac Miller's heirs
Michael Miller's heirs
Oliver Miller, lives in Balt Co
Morris Millhouse's heirs, lays in Pa
Mary Ann Misline
David Mitchell
John Mitchell, belongs to a minor
Thos. Morris
Samuel Mount, lives in Va
Thos. Mullineux, lives in Balt Co
Philip Murphey's heirs
Christian Myers
Ralph Neall, lives in St.
William Needham, he is

Sarah Needham, she is dead
Christian New
Margaret Newsbaume
John Nicholls Junr, gone to Va
Thos. Noble's heirs, possessors live
    in PG Co
William O'Neill
Laurence O'Neill (addl)
Thos. Ogle Senr, lives in Cecil Co
John Oliver, a stroller
John Jas. Owen, gone to Va
Joshua Owen, lives in Balt Co
Geo. Pack's heirs
Hugh Parker's heirs, possessor lives
    in Pa
Richard Parnall, lives in AA Co
James Patterson, lives in Pa
John Pearce, man run away
Thos. Pecker's heirs (minors)
Joseph Perry
Robert Peter (addl)
Elias Petitt, runaway
Thos. Philpott; lives in London
William Pidgeon, lives in Pa
John Christian Pinkley
David Pott's heirs, they live in Va
William Powell, man run
Peter Praigg
John Smith Prather's heirs
Thos. Clagett Prather's heirs; he is
    at Red Stone (sole heir)
Elders of Presbyterian House
Casper Primore
John Radford
Goslip Ratt
John Ray, lives in AA Co
Andrew Reid
Nicholas Rhoads, is a mad man, no
    effects
John Richards
Benjamin Riddle
Henry Ridenour
John Ridgely, live in Balt Co
Mary Ridgway, alias Ridgely
John Riester, lives in Balt Co
John Riley
Valentine Rinehart
Daniel Robbins, land in Pa
John Robbins, lives in Va
William Roberts
Anthony Roof
John Harmon Rosenplatt

Doctr David Ross, lands in Pa
William Rugdon, lives in Pa
Thos Rutland, lives in AA Co
Alexander Rutter
John Sammons
John Sausar, run away
Andrew Scott's hrs
John Semple, lives in Va
William Sergeant
John Settern's heirs
Horatio Sharp; Fort Frederick stands
    on this land
Isaac Shelby (addl)
David Shelby, lives in Pa
John Shepherd's heirs, live in Va
Laurence Shock
David Shriver (addl)
Michael Shultz
Andrew Simpson, lives in Pa
Geo. Sly, is dead
Joseph Smith
Philip Smith
Richard Smith
John Smith's hrs
Peter Snider
Doctor Henry Snively
Richard Snowden's heirs
Frederick Sower
Conrod Space(?)
William Sparks
Jeremiah Spires gone to Carolina
Joseph Sprigg
Gilbert Sprigg's heirs, heirs live in
    PG Co
Col. Edward Sprigg's heirs, heirs
    live in PG Co
Ozburn Sprigg's heirs, land belongs
    to minors
James Spurgeon, lives and has pt of
    his land in Pa
William Spurgeon, lives in Pa
Henry Stall
Geo. Stanier
Thos. Stansbury
Simon Stickle
Andrew Stigar, lives in Balt Co
Thos. Stoddert's heirs, they live in
    PG Co
Henry Stole
John Stoner's heirs; the heir
    Pa
William Stroope, lives in Va

Rent Due on land in Frederick County, 1768-1769

John Hance Stullman
Edward Swaney
Alexander and Andrew Symmer's
  asignees
Thos. Talbert, lives in PG Co
Geo. Taylor
Richard Tedd's heirs, a poor man, no
  effects
Samuel Thomas
Christopher Thomas, man in Carolina
Anthony Thompson
Cornelius & Ann Thompson
John Thompson's heirs
Capt. William Tipple, lives in London
Joseph Tomblinson, lays in Pa
Caleb Touchstone
Alexander Tracey, man in Carolina
Goodheart Trisler
John Trundle
Samuel Tulaghpan(?)
Robt Twigg, lives in Pa
Peter Ulamer
Christian Valentine
Richard Vandike, lives in Pa
Daniel Vears' heirs
Jeremiah Virgin
Hancy Waggoner
James Waling Senr
Zachariah Walker
William Wallace's heirs
Jacob Walter
Edward Ward
Joseph Ward, lives in Calvert Co
Alexander Warfield's heirs, they live
  in AA Co
Bazil Warfield, lives on the Eastern
  Shore
James Warford, is in Carolina
Joseph Warford, land and man in Pa
John Waters (addl)
Samuel Waters, a stroller
Nathan Waters, lives in AA Co
John Watts, lives in Pa
John Webbster & Compy, they live in
  Balt Co
William Welch, is dead, no effects on
  land
Benjamin Welch, lives in AA Co
Alexander Wells, lives in Balt Co
Bernard Wertenburgh, lives in PG Co
William West's heirs
John White, gone to Carolina

Abram Whitmon and others
Peter Wiesinger
John Wiles
William Wilkins
Edward Willet
Thos. Willett
Ninian Willett (addl)
Tobias Stansburg's heirs, live in
  Balt Co
William Starr, in Carolina
Elisha Williams
John Williams Junr
James Williamson
Thos. Willson
William Willson
Thos. Wilson
John Wilson, he lives in PG Co
Geo. Winder
Jacob Wise, gone to Carolina
Jane Wivell
Peter Yeater
James Young
Notley Young
John Youngblood
Henry Younger

Petition for Road

From the Judgements records of 1749, Frederick County:

"Sundry of the Inhabitants of Linganore and Sams Creek preferr to ... necessity of a road to be cleared from the Chaple which the sd Inhabitants is now building between the Drafts of Linganore and the Drafts of Sams Creek to the main Waggon Road from Annapolis to Fredk Town and to fall in to sd road neer Mr. Edward and Willm. Bettys... Signed: John Phillips, Joseph Wood, John Carmack, Jno. Howard son of Gideon, Phillip Howard Juner, Stephen Richards, Pattrick Holligan (his mark), Daniel Sings, Daniel Ryan, Darby Ryan, William Carmack, John Justice Junr, Thos. Wiles, Rubin Phillips, John Williams, Jacob Nicholads, John Willes, Arch'l Cambill, John Justis Senior, Mounst Justice, James Brown, Mathyas Stallcup, Robert Burchfield, Solomon Sparks, James Mackdanl, William Lacefield, Charles Wood, John Brightwell, Richard Combs Senr, Richard Combs Juner, Denis Ensey."

This petition was granted. Major Henry Munday and Captain and John Middagh were appointed to "view the places and lay out the roads."

INDEX

www.ingramcontent.com/pod-product-compliance
Lightning Source LLC
Chambersburg PA
CBHW081528040426

42447CB00013B/3381